Constance Milburn

DINOSAURS

KENNETH GORDON SCHOOL

Illustrated by Colin Newman

PUFFIN BOOKS

Words in **bold** type are explained in the glossary on p.30.

How to say the dinosaurs' names is explained in the text.

Contents

What was a dinosaur? 4
Finding out about dinosaurs 6
Dinosaur remains 8
The first dinosaurs 10
The discovery of the dinosaurs 12
Beast-footed dinosaurs 14
Plant-eating dinosaurs 16
Reptile-footed dinosaurs 18
Bird-footed dinosaurs 20
Horned dinosaurs 22
The largest horned dinosaur 24
The ancestor of birds 26
Why dinosaurs became extinct 28

Glossary 30
Books to read 31
How to find out more 31
Index 32

What was a dinosaur?

What was a dinosaur? A dinosaur was a **reptile** that lived millions of years ago. But what is a reptile? Reptiles are animals like lizards, snakes, turtles and crocodiles. They have a dry skin of scales or horny plates. All reptiles hatch from eggs.

Pteranodon

Stegosaurus

Finding out about dinosaurs

Scientists know what sort of rocks dinosaur bones can be found in. They search for these kinds of rocks and if they discover them they look for dinosaur **remains**.

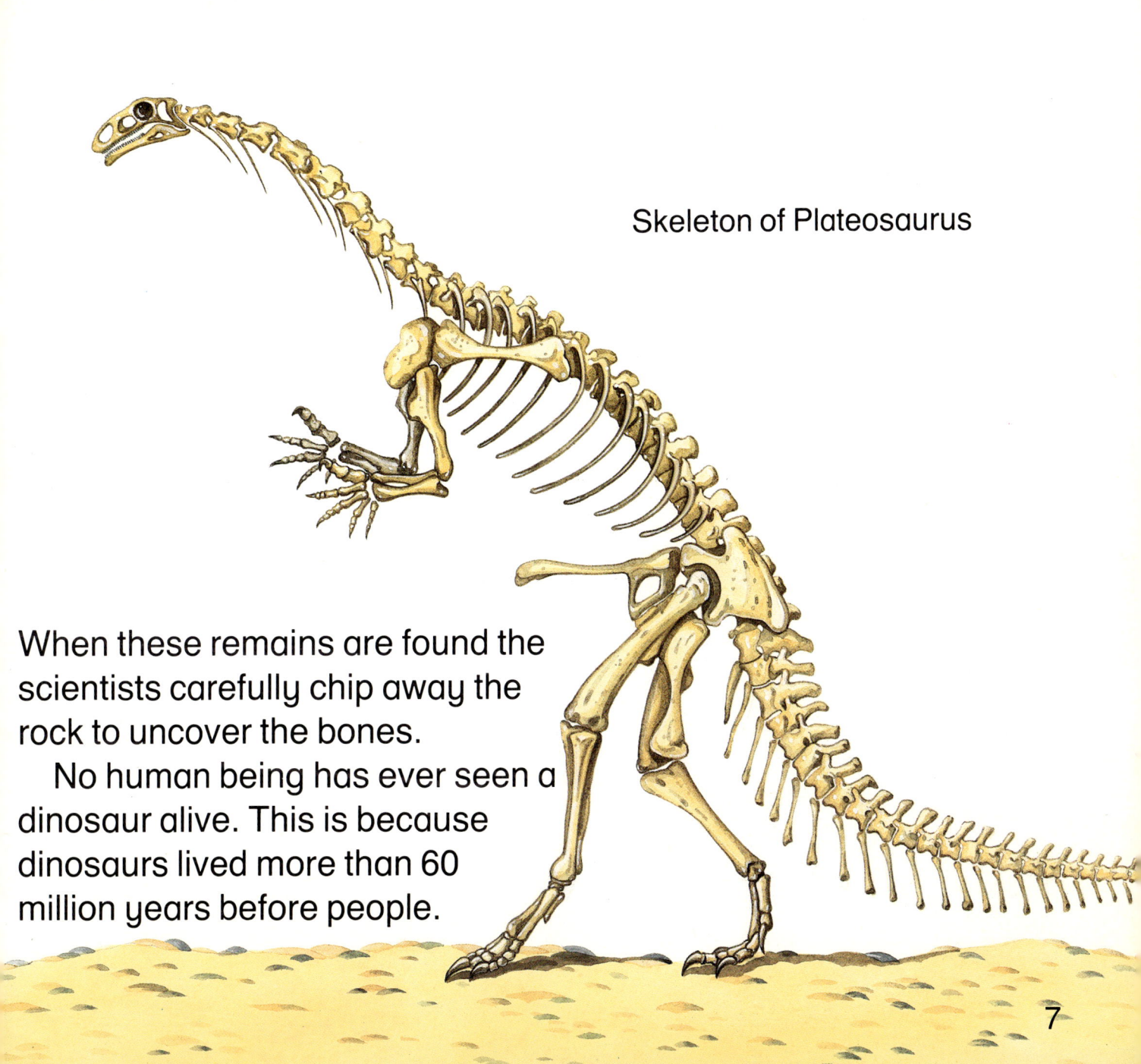

Skeleton of Plateosaurus

When these remains are found the scientists carefully chip away the rock to uncover the bones.

No human being has ever seen a dinosaur alive. This is because dinosaurs lived more than 60 million years before people.

Dinosaur remains

Remains of dinosaurs have been found in different parts of the world. When scientists find a part of a dinosaur they work out what the whole dinosaur looked like.

A foot-print of a dinosaur found in the Arizona desert, USA.

In China scientists were very lucky. They found a whole **skeleton** of Yang-chu-ano-saurus! The scientists looked carefully at the way it was lying. They worked out that Yangchuanosaurus could bend its neck, lift its tail and take long **strides** when it was hunting for food.

Yangchuanosaurus

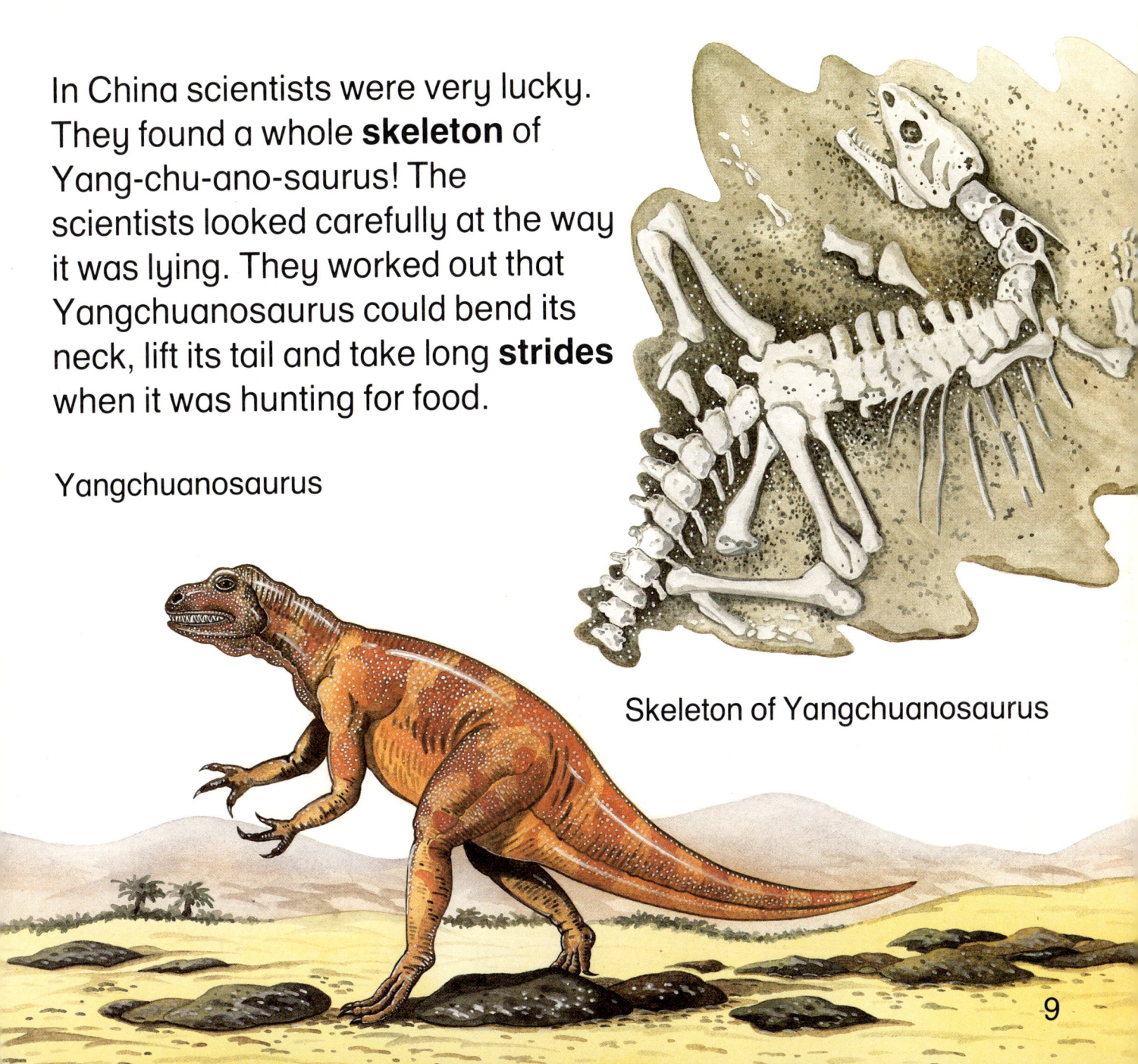

Skeleton of Yangchuanosaurus

The first dinosaurs

The first dinosaurs were small animals. They looked rather like lizards. They lived in rivers and fed on fishes and insects. Then they grew strong tails and long back legs to help them to swim. Thousands of years passed. Slowly they grew into bigger animals more like crocodiles. Then they began to come on land looking for food.

Their back legs were much stronger and longer than their front legs. This made it difficult for them to move quickly on land. The first dinosaurs ran on just their back legs. They used their tails to help them keep upright.

The discovery of the dinosaurs

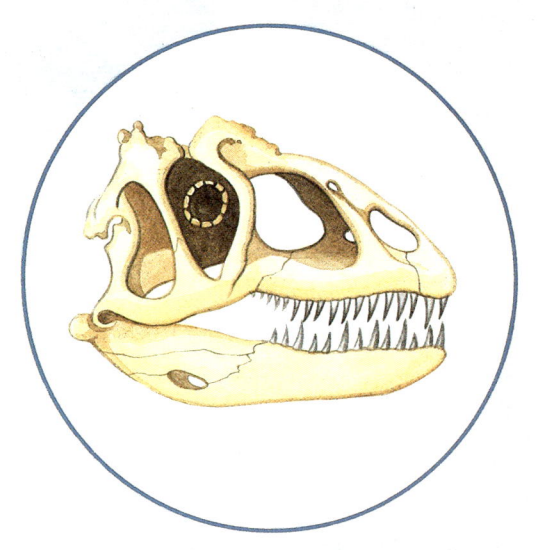

The first dinosaur remains to be discovered by people were found in England. They belonged to Mega-lo-saurus. Megalosaurus means 'great reptile' or 'big lizard'.

Look at the teeth of Megalosaurus in this skull. Megalosaurus was a meat-eating dinosaur which ran on two legs.

Megalosaurus

Megalosaurus had a big head and rows of large, sharp teeth. It used its clawed feet to attack its **prey**.

Beast-footed dinosaurs

All the meat-eating dinosaurs which walked upright on two feet were called **beast**-footed dinosaurs. The hands and feet usually had sharp claws for tearing meat.

Ty-rann-o-saurus Rex was the largest meat-eating dinosaur. Its name means 'king of the **tyrant** reptiles'. Tyrannosaurus could not catch its prey so it fed on animal remains and small dinosaurs.

Tyrannosaurus Rex

This skeleton of Tyrannosaurus stands in the American Museum of Natural History in New York.

Brachiosaurus

Plant-eating dinosaurs

Slowly the dinosaurs changed. Many became plant-eaters. Some of them grew to enormous sizes.

Brach-i-o-saurus was a plant-eater and one of the largest land animals ever to have lived on earth. Can you see that the front legs are longer than the back legs? Brachiosaurus spent a lot of time walking in **swamps** and lakes, eating plants.

Reptile-footed dinosaurs

Some dinosaurs were called reptile-footed. Brach-i-o-saurus was a reptile-footed dinosaur. Because Brachiosaurus was big and heavy it walked on all fours.

All the reptile-footed dinosaurs had small heads and long necks like Bron-to-saurus. Brontosaurus means 'thunder lizard'.

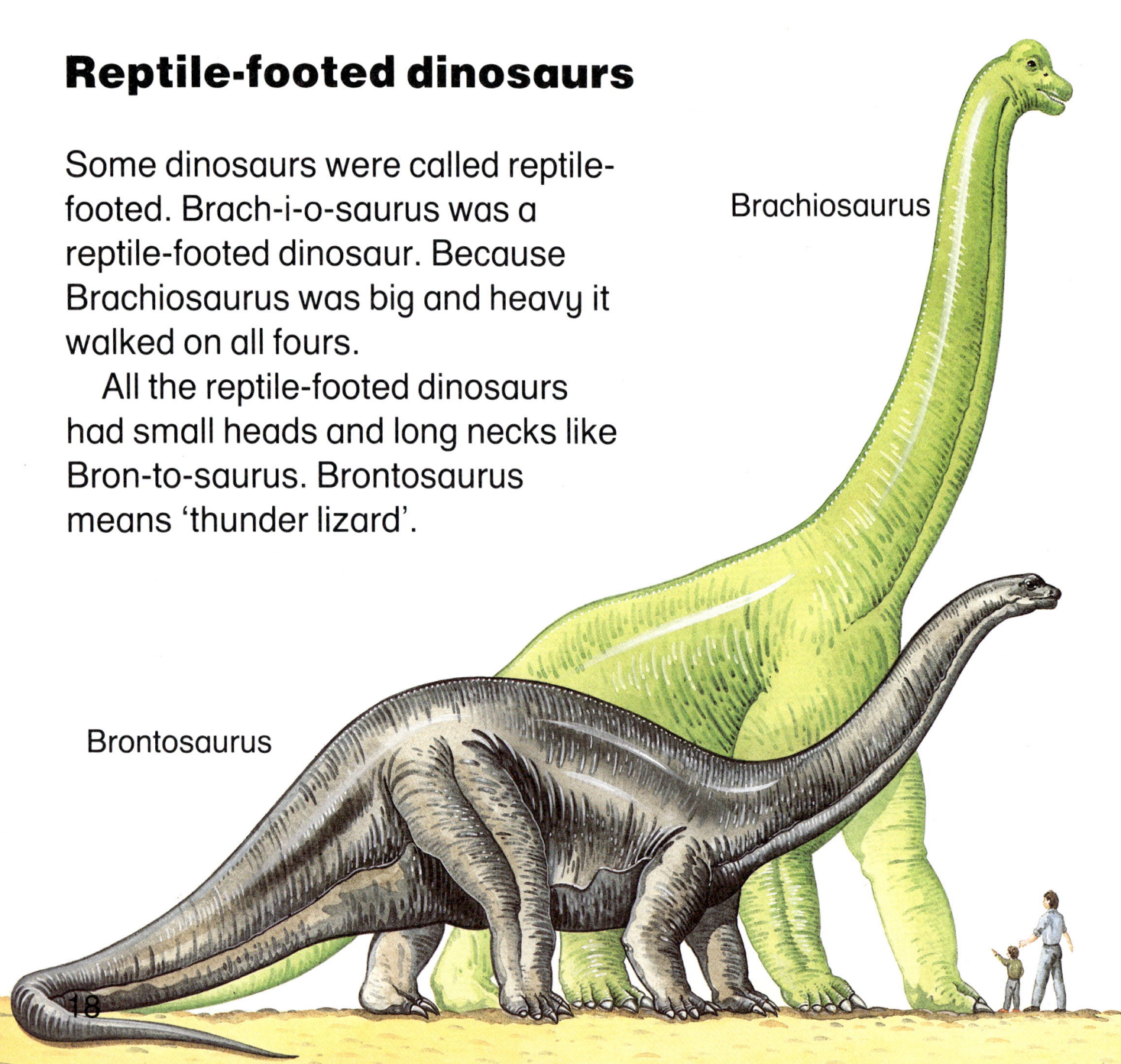

Brachiosaurus

Brontosaurus

These dinosaurs lived in **herds**. They spent a lot of time in swamps looking for food but they always laid their eggs on land. When the herd moved, the younger, smaller dinosaurs travelled in the middle of the herd. This meant that the meat-eating dinosaurs could not get them.

A herd of Brontosaurus

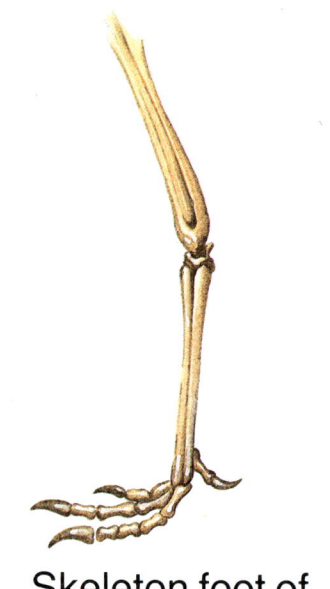

Skeleton foot of Heterodontosaurus

Heterodontosaurus

Bird-footed dinosaurs

As well as beast-footed and reptile-footed there were also bird-footed dinosaurs. They had feet rather like those of a bird. Look at the skeleton foot of Het-ero-don-to-saurus. Heterodontosaurus was a small dinosaur, less than 1 metre tall.

Many bird-footed dinosaurs grew very big like Ig-u-ano-don. Iguanodon walked on its back legs but would stand on all fours when feeding. Bird-footed dinosaurs were plant-eaters.

Iguanodon

Horned dinosaurs

Some dinosaurs had horns. Others had a frill at the back of the neck. Horned dinosaurs had strong teeth and jaws. They could eat very tough plants like the palm **fronds** shown in the picture.

Pro-to-cera-tops means 'first horned face'.

Protoceratops

Protoceratops walked on all fours and ate plants. The female dinosaur laid about twelve eggs in a nest. Then she covered them with sand. Protoceratops did not go far away from the eggs until they were hatched. Why do you think she kept guard on her eggs?

The largest horned dinosaur

Tri-cera-tops means 'three horned face'. Herds of Triceratops lived in North America. Triceratops was a big, heavy dinosaur with three horns and a mouth shaped like a parrot's beak. Triceratops walked on all fours and ate trees and plants.

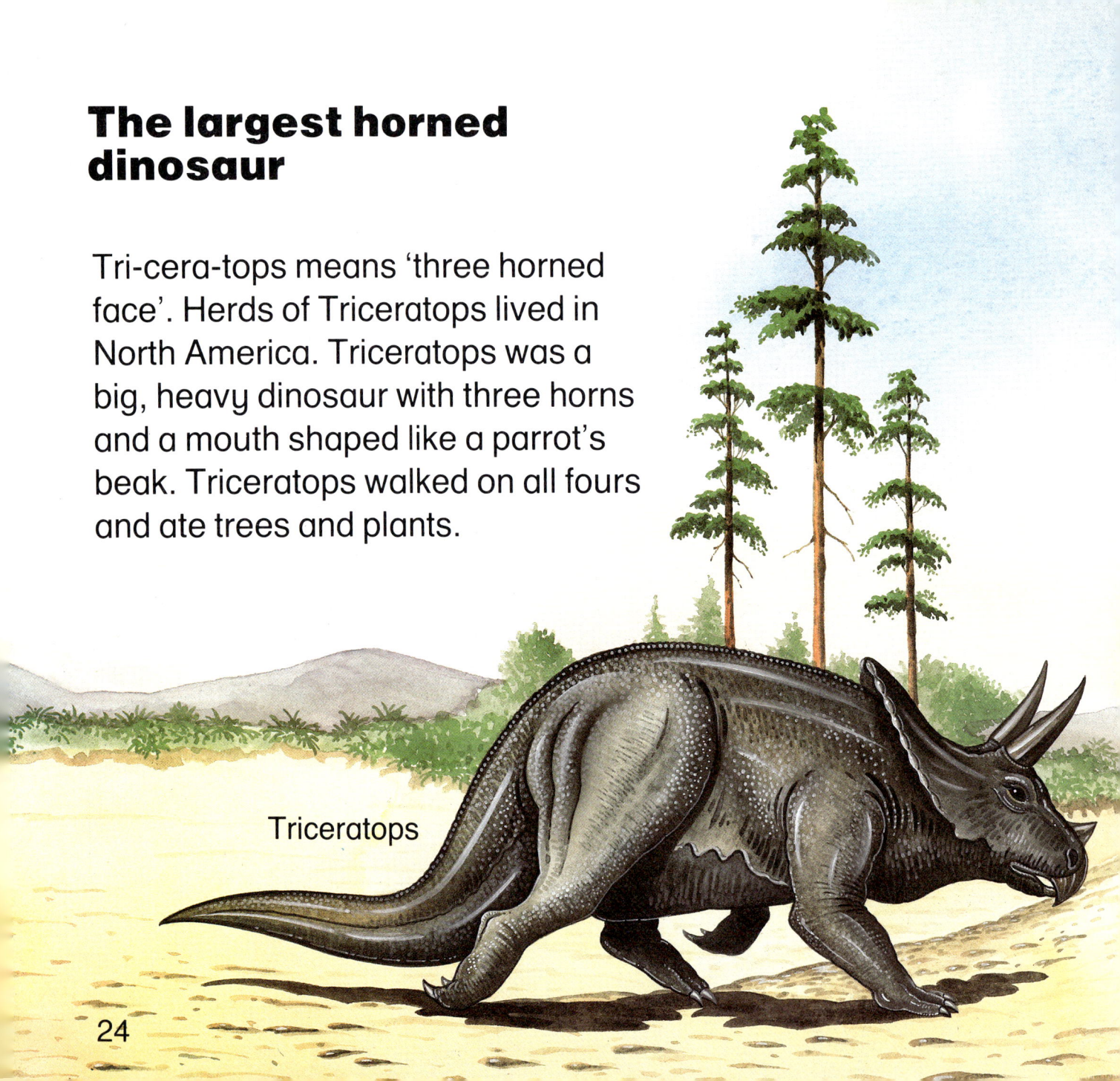

Triceratops

Horned dinosaurs fought by locking their horns together and pushing each other until one gave in. Triceratops was the largest of the horned dinosaurs.

The ancestor of birds

Ar-chae-op-teryx was a very important dinosaur because it was the **ancestor** of birds. Archaeopteryx had feathers and could **glide** using its wings. When it was on the ground Archaeopteryx tucked its wings into its sides and ran on two legs just like our birds do today.

Archaeopteryx

Why dinosaurs became extinct

Dinosaurs did not suddenly disappear. It took 500 thousand years for them to become **extinct**. Many people think that a giant **meteor** from outer space struck the earth. The cloud of dust from this shut out the sun's rays. This caused the death of plants. Without food the larger animals died.

Another idea is that the **temperature** on earth changed and the dinosaurs could not live in it. No one is really sure why dinosaurs disappeared. Perhaps one day we will find out why dinosaurs became extinct.

Glossary

Ancestor A relative who lived a long time ago.
Beast Any animal other than people.
Extinct Animals and plants that used to live on this planet but have now died out.
Fronds The leaves of a palm tree.
Glide Travel through the air on outstretched wings.
Herd A large group of animals living and feeding together.
Meteor A lump of rock which falls to earth from space.
Prey An animal hunted or caught by another for food.
Remains Parts of a dead body or skeleton.
Reptile An animal with a dry, scaly, skin which lays eggs with shells.
Skeleton The set of bones in a body.
Strides Big steps.
Swamps Waterlogged ground which is usually overgrown with lots of plants.
Temperature A measure of hot and cold.
Tyrant A cruel king or ruler with unlimited power.

Books to read

Dinosaurs, Small World Series, Henry Pluckrose (Hamish Hamilton, 1979)
Dinosaurs, A First Look Book, David Lambert (Franklin Watts, 1982)
The Age of the Dinosaurs, David Norman (Wayland, 1985)
The Superbook of Dinosaurs, Ron Taylor (Kingfisher Books, 1985)

How to find out more

If you want to know more about dinosaurs visit your nearest natural history museum. There may be a fossil-collecting club or society that you can join in your area. Your local library will have information about this, and will also have other books about dinosaurs that you can borrow.

Index

A Archaeopteryx   26

B Bones   6
  Brachiosaurus   16, 18
  Brontosaurus   18

C China   9

D Dinosaurs:
  Beast-footed   14, 20
  Bird-footed   20, 21
  Horned   22, 24, 25
  Meat-eating   14, 19
  Plant-eating   16, 21
  Reptile-footed   18, 20

E Eggs   4, 23
  England   12
  Eryops   10
  Euparkeria   11
  Extinction   28

G Giant Dragonfly   10

H Heterodontosaurus   20
  Hylonomous   11

I Ichthyostega   10
  Iguanodon   21

M Megalosaurus   12
  Meteor   28

N North America   24

O Outer space   28

P Plateosaurus   7
  Protoceratops   22

R Reptiles   4, 14, 18, 20

S Scientists   6, 8
  Stegosaurus   4

T Triceratops   24
  Tyrannosaurus Rrex   14

Y Yangchuanosaurus   9

Picture acknowledgements
The photographs in this book were supplied by: Bruce Coleman (by Sullivan and Rogers) 8; Trans. No. V/C 2143 Courtesy Department Library Services American Museum of Natural History 15.